FUN FACTS

Ripley's

Believe It or Not!®

Kids

& SILLY STORIES

PLAY IT LOUD!

RIPLEY
PUBLISHING
a Jim Pattison Company

What's Inside!

Amazing Animals!

An Explosive Treat!

Chilling Stories!

CHECK THIS OUT!

Really?
Glowing chameleons

No Way!
Lava lake

Cute
Pet aardvark

Crazy
Chocolate Dress

Wow!
Dragon bridge

MONSTER CAFE

The Kawaii Monster Cafe in Harajuku, Japan, has colorful themed rooms showcasing the best of kawaii culture.

Kawaii

(KAH-wah-ee)
means "cute"
in Japanese
(可愛い).
It also is the
culture of cuteness
in Japan.

STRANGE SPORTS

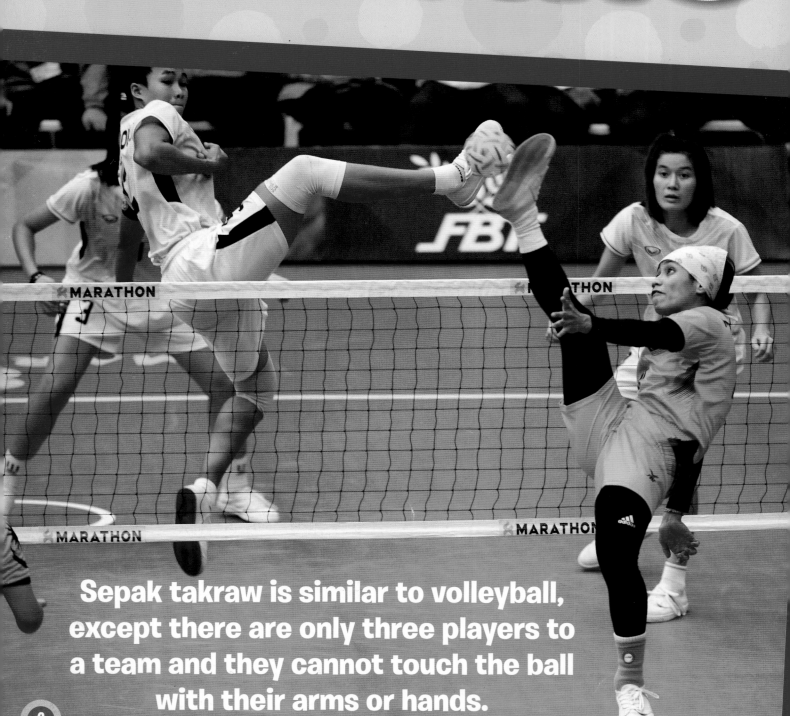

Sepak takraw is similar to volleyball, except there are only three players to a team and they cannot touch the ball with their arms or hands.

Popular in Germany, eisfussball is a bizarre cross between soccer and hockey.

Slamball is a full-contact version of basketball played on trampolines!

The official sport of Colorado is pack burro (donkey) racing.

Fun & Games!

Which shadow perfectly matches the sepak takraw player?

Spot the 7 differences between these two scenes!

Want to see how you did?
Turn to pages 88-90 for the solutions!

Dimensional Drawings

Stefan Pabst of Hamburg, Germany, creates paintings that seem to pop right off of the paper!

The art must be viewed from certain angles for the 3-D illusion to appear.

THAT'S (NOT) NUTS!

Macadamia nuts fall off the tree when they are ready to be eaten.

Cashews are related to poison ivy and must be cooked to remove toxic irritants!

Almonds, cashews, and Brazil nuts are all technically seeds, not nuts!

Humans have been eating walnuts for at least 9,000 years.

In different parts of the world, the pistachio is known as the "smiling nut" or the "happy nut."

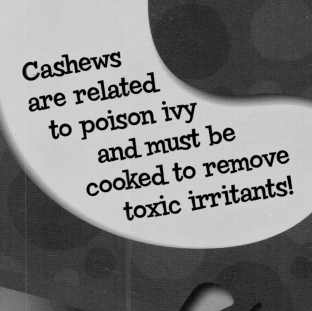

In the Garden

This patch of sea grass swaying gently in a current is actually a colony of garden eels!

They hunt by sitting and waiting for food to float by, like this unlucky krill!

Build It BIG!

Every year during the holiday season, the city of Gävle, Sweden, builds a 43-foot-tall goat made of straw.

The Dragon Bridge in Da Nang City, Vietnam, is 2,185 feet long and can shoot fire and water from its mouth!

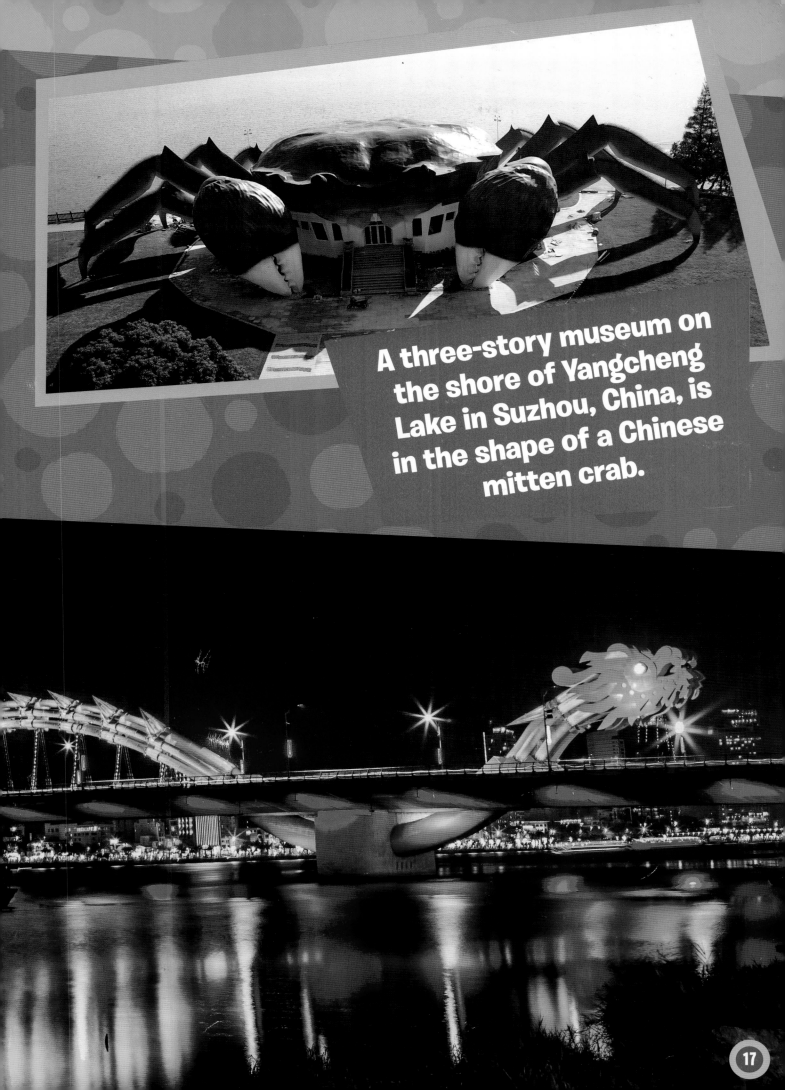

A three-story museum on the shore of Yangcheng Lake in Suzhou, China, is in the shape of a Chinese mitten crab.

Macaron Match

It takes Melissa six hours to create the sheep.

Melissa Huang of Toronto, Canada, bakes macarons in the shapes of plants, animals, and even other foods!

Find the two macarons that match each other perfectly.

Want to see how you did?
Turn to pages 88-90 for the solutions!

Macaron
(MA-kah-rown):
a small, chewy
cookie sandwich
with a sweet filling.

Tree-lieve It or Not!

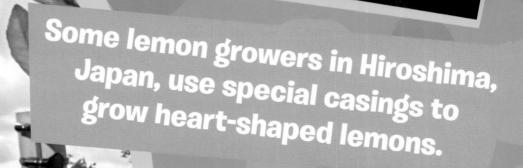

Some lemon growers in Hiroshima, Japan, use special casings to grow heart-shaped lemons.

A school in Beijing, China, has a 100-year-old tree growing in the middle of its soccer field!

A tree grows through the kitchen and roof of Kit Kat restaurant in Toronto, Canada. Legend has it, the tree grants wishes to those who touch it.

ANIMAL ANATOMY

Newfoundland dogs have webbed toes.

A lobster's bladder is in its head.

Squirrels can rotate their hind feet 180 degrees, allowing them to climb headfirst down trees.

The saiga antelope uses its large nose to heat up and filter the air it breathes.

Nautiluses can have up to 90 arms, all covered in a sticky substance and tiny hairs used to trap food.

The jerboa can leap 10 feet, despite being only 6 inches tall!

North American porcupines are covered in 30,000 sharp quills.

A giraffe's upper lip is prehensile, meaning it is capable of grabbing like a hand.

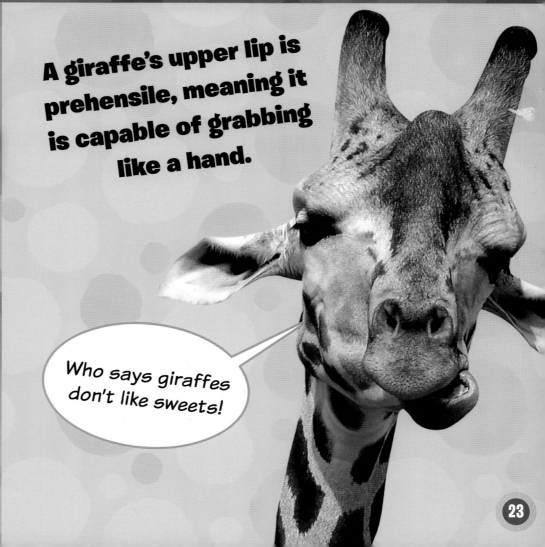

Who says giraffes don't like sweets!

In the Heights

Louise and Samuel were part of the "Highline Extreme" yearly event.

Daredevils Louise Lenoble and Samuel Volery performed stunts between two cable cars on the mountain of Moleson in Switzerland.

Lava Lake

Bubbling in a giant crater on Mount Nyiragongo in the Democratic Republic of the Congo is a lava lake 820 feet across.

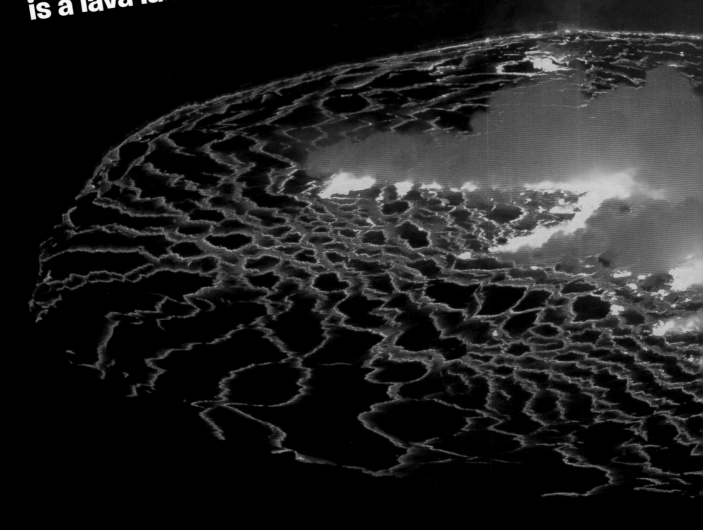

The lava lake in Mount Nyiragongo is the world's largest, once recorded to be almost 2,000 feet deep!

Jupiter's moon Io is the most volcanically active place in the solar system.

Chocolate Lava Mug Cake

A culinary school in Senayan City, Indonesia, baked a cake that was 108.27 feet tall and weighed 20 tons!

ingredients

2 TBS butter, melted and cooled

1 egg

3 TBS milk

3 TBS flour

4 TBS sugar

2 TBS unsweetened cocoa powder

¼ tsp vanilla

1 pinch of salt

3 TBS chocolate chips

In 2014, a group at Syracuse University in New York cooked steaks and roasted marshmallows over man-made lava.

1 In a large coffee mug, mix together the butter, egg, and milk.

2 Stir in the sugar and flour, and then the cocoa, vanilla, and salt.

3 Add the chocolate chips.

4 Microwave the batter-filled mug for 2 minutes; then wait a few minutes for the cake to cool.

Optional: Top your cake with ice cream, fresh fruit, or whipped cream!

Feathered Friends

Rudy the Pekin duck and Barclay the golden retriever became unlikely best friends after Barclay kept trying to steal food from Rudy's coop!

Pigeons sometimes backflip while flying, and no one is sure why.

Kyoto Ohata of Tokyo, Japan, designed these felt pigeon pumps so she wouldn't scare the birds away as she walks by.

This seagull at Cannon Beach, Oregon, was caught stuffing its beak with a sea star and then swallowing it whole!

FACE OFF

A photographer spotted a smiling face within volcanic lava in the Afar region of Ethiopia, Africa.

Humans are quick to see faces and familiar shapes in unexpected places thanks to a phenomenon known as "pareidolia" (pare-eye-doh-lia).

You've seen the man in the Moon before, but what about Mickey Mouse on Mercury?

Check out this ghostly face on Mars!

Do you see the face formed in the rocks? This amazing natural formation is in Ebihens, France.

Face VALUE

Copy some of these wacky facial features to build a funny face!

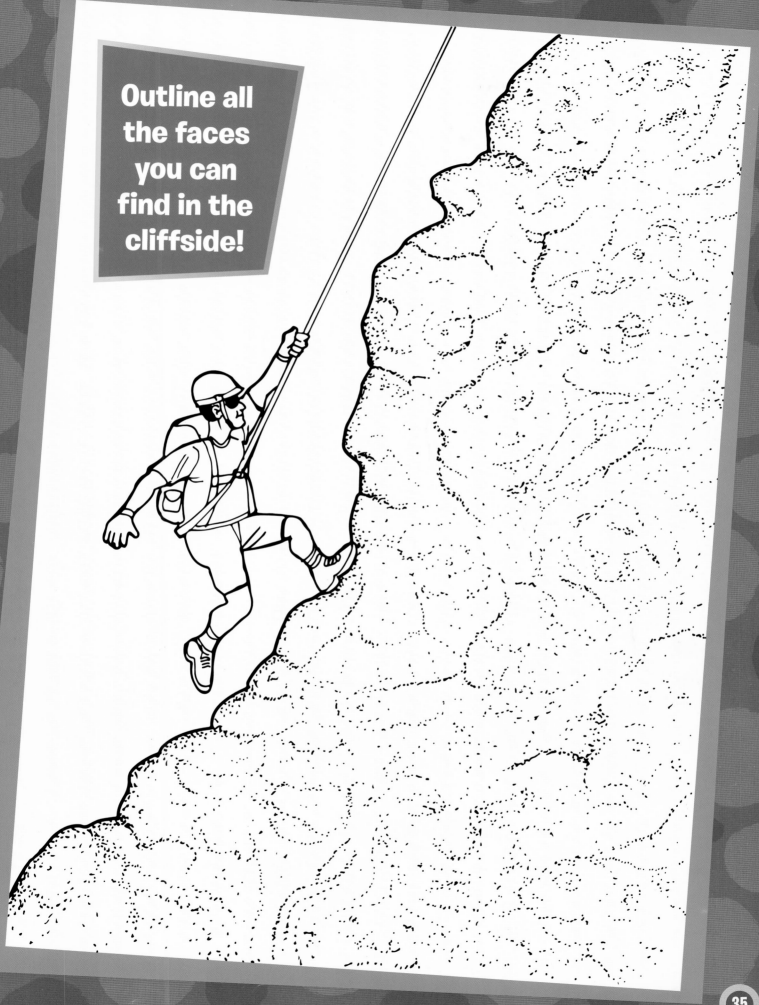

Outline all the faces you can find in the cliffside!

35

How do you SLEEP?

The Null Stern hotel in Switzerland is just an open-air room atop a mountain, with a bed and nightstand with lamps.

ZZZ

Humans spend about 25 years of their life sleeping.

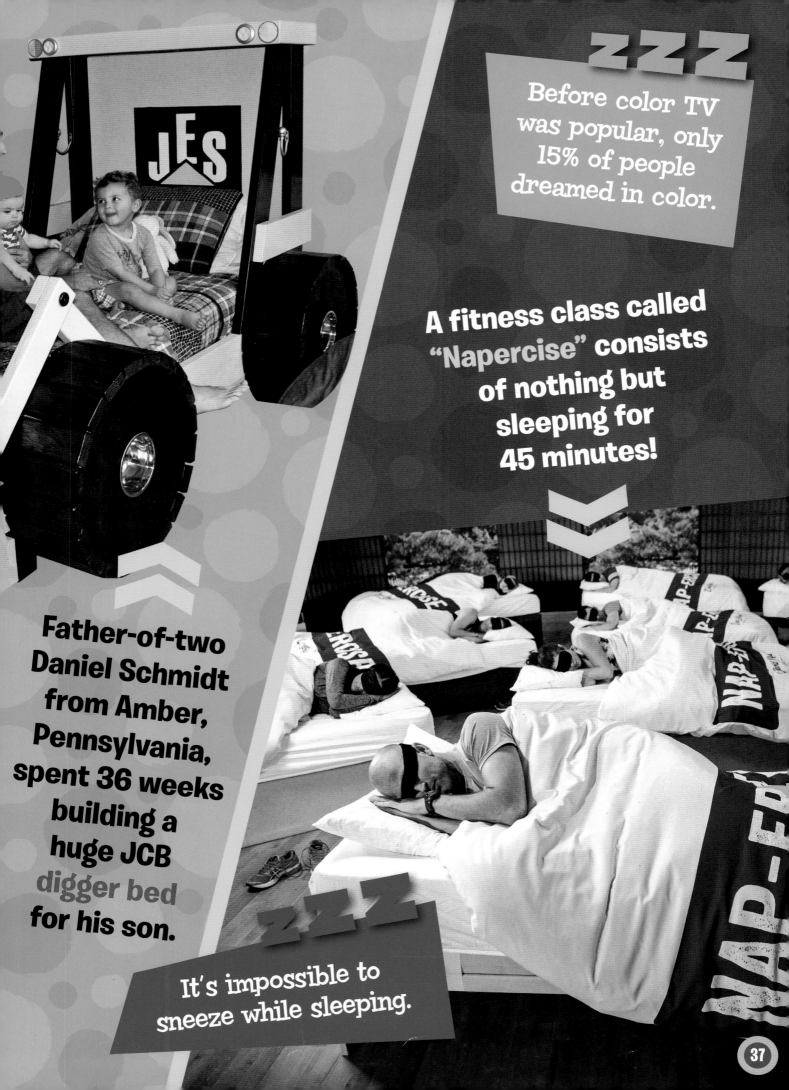

ZZZ

Before color TV was popular, only 15% of people dreamed in color.

A fitness class called "Napercise" consists of nothing but sleeping for 45 minutes!

Father-of-two Daniel Schmidt from Amber, Pennsylvania, spent 36 weeks building a huge JCB digger bed for his son.

It's impossible to sneeze while sleeping.

GIANT GRAFFITI

Contos (COHN-tuss) means "stories" in Portuguese.

Luna Buschinelli, 19, painted this massive mural in Rio de Janeiro, Brazil.

The artwork, titled *Contos*, is nearly 27,000 square feet in size!

WINTER WONDERLAND

Ice climbers Mathis Dumas and Jeff Mercier climbed up the inside of this 164-foot-tall ice tube near Mont Blanc in France.

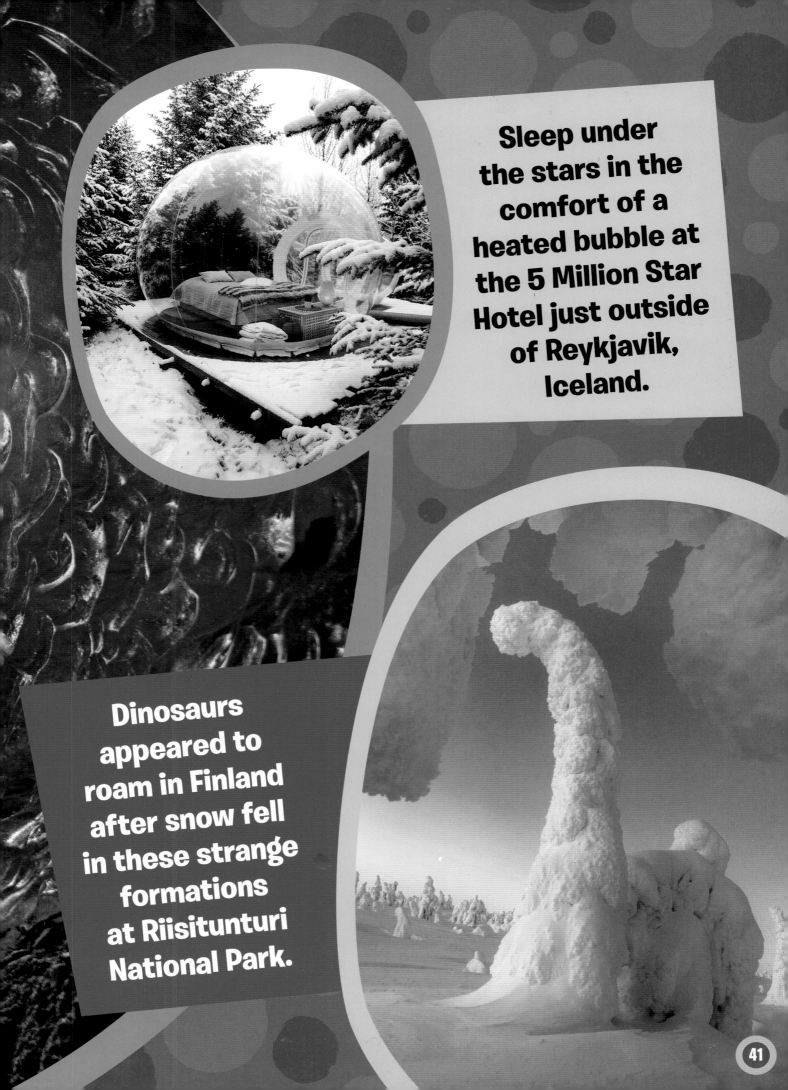

Sleep under the stars in the comfort of a heated bubble at the 5 Million Star Hotel just outside of Reykjavik, Iceland.

Dinosaurs appeared to roam in Finland after snow fell in these strange formations at Riisitunturi National Park.

Snow Way!

Bulgarian photographer Georgi Slavov captured these stunning images of super-small snowflakes.

Snowflakes are categorized into 35 different shapes.

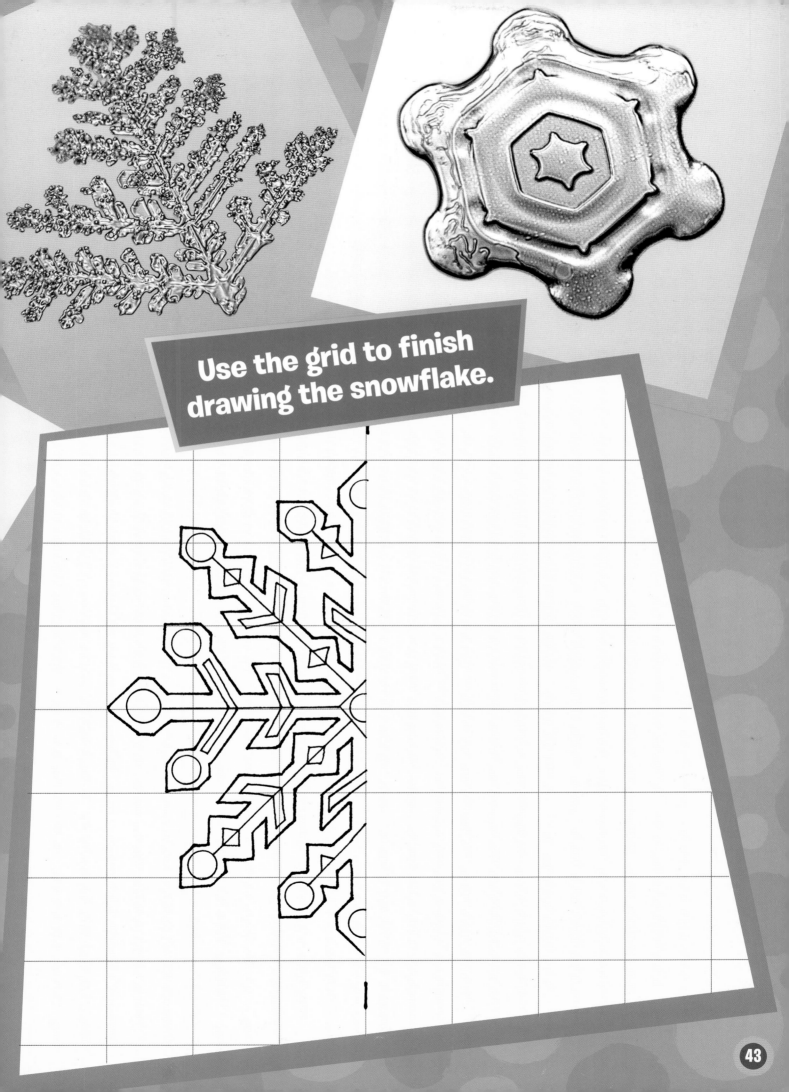

Use the grid to finish drawing the snowflake.

Pretty in Pink

Pink, white, and purple shibazakura blossoms blanket the hills of Higashimokoto Shibazakura Park in Ōzora, Japan.

Shibazakura
(SHE-bahzah-koo-rah)
is also known as
moss phlox, and is
a ground-covering
plant that blooms for
about a month near
the end of spring.

Sky High

Over the state of Arizona in October 2017, a group of 217 skydivers jumped from a total of 10 planes.

JUMPING FOR JOY!

Take turns with a friend asking for words to fill in the blanks in the story below. When you're done, read it out loud!

Last weekend I went skydiving at _____. Since it was
                                                    place

my first time _____ out of a plane, I needed to go
                      verb ending in -ing

with a _____ instructor. Imagine my surprise when I
              adjective

found out my instructor was _____! Next thing I knew,
                            person

we were in the plane, _____ high above _____.
                    verb ending in -ing   **noun**

I looked out the window and saw _____ _____
                              plural noun   **verb ending in -ing**

through the clouds—it was _____! When the
                          adjective

moment came to _____, my instructor shouted,
                  verb

"Let's _____ this _____" before _____ me
       verb   **noun**   **verb ending in -ing**

out of the open door! As we fell, we _____ and enjoyed
                        verb ending in -ed

the view of _____ below us. We landed _____
          noun   **adverb**

on the ground, where _____ took our picture with a
                  person

_____. I'm going again this weekend!
  noun

PLAY IT

Music may be able to make flowers grow faster.

The word "music" comes from the Muses, goddesses of the arts in Greek mythology.

Leo Fender, inventor of the Telecaster and Stratocaster, could not play the guitar.

"Ukulele" means "jumping flea" in Hawaiian.

LOUD!

Your **heartbeat** changes and mimics the music you listen to.

The song "Jingle Bells" was originally written for Thanksgiving.

Music, painting, poetry, literature, and architecture all used to be part of the modern **Olympic Games** from 1912 to 1948.

A song that gets stuck in your head is called an "earworm."

FACE THE MUSIC!

How many smaller words can you make out of the phrase below? Words must have four letters or more.

ARE YOU READY TO ROCK?

Follow the wires to find out which guitarist is connected to the amp!

Want to see how you did?
Turn to pages 88-90 for the solutions!

HEADS UP

The residents of Chongqing, China, were visited by the Teenage Mutant Ninja Turtles in the form of these playful sculptures.

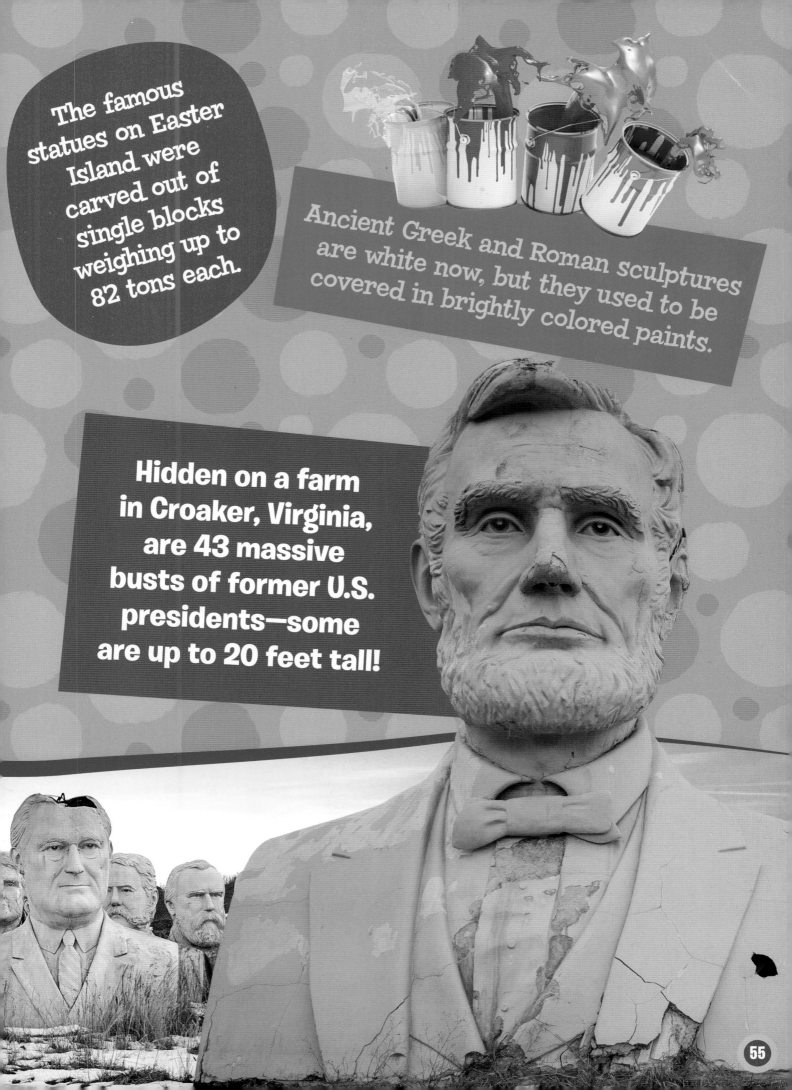

The famous statues on Easter Island were carved out of single blocks weighing up to 82 tons each.

Ancient Greek and Roman sculptures are white now, but they used to be covered in brightly colored paints.

Hidden on a farm in Croaker, Virginia, are 43 massive busts of former U.S. presidents—some are up to 20 feet tall!

Dress to Impress

Emily Seilhamer of Elizabethtown, Pennsylvania, made this dress using Starburst candy wrappers and elastic thread.

A model walks down the runway in a dress decorated with chocolate at the 2017 Beirut Cooking Festival in Lebanon.

These dresses are made out of Post-it Notes!

From the Depths

This lobster caught by Alex Todd of Maine looks like it's made of crystal, but it actually has leucism.

Leucism (LEW-sism) is a genetic condition that reduces dark colors in animals.

Sound travels faster in water than in air.

Oceans make up 70% of the Earth's surface.

A fisherman off the coast of California was shocked when he reeled in a lingcod with a whole octopus in its mouth!

Colors disappear the deeper you go underwater—red is the first to go.

What a HOOT

Owls can't digest fur, bones, feathers, or scales, so they later regurgitate a compacted pellet in the shape of their gizzard

Owls cannot rotate their heads 360 degrees. They can, however, turn their necks 270 degrees.

Barn owls have heart-shaped faces.

The smallest owl is the elf owl, which sometimes makes its home in the giant saguaro cactus, nesting in holes made by other animals.

Owls are nearly silent when they fly.

Owls can hear prey under leaves, plants, dirt, and snow.

ONE FELL SWOOP

Using the clues, locate the word on the crisscross grid. We've placed one to get you started!

3 letters
owl
fly
egg

4 letters
nest
tree
prey
hoot
beak

5 letters
talon
owlet

6 letters
pellet
hunter
silent
wisdom

7 letters
rodents
gizzard
habitat

8 letters
feathers

9 letters
nocturnal

11 letters
regurgitate
carnivorous

'TIS THE SEASON

Ginkgo trees are the same now as they were 200 million years ago!

Joanna Hedrick, a counselor at Sacramento State University in California, rakes beautiful patterns into the fallen ginkgo tree leaves on the school's campus.

This house in Webster, New York, was frozen solid after high winds covered it in waves from Lake Ontario.

To welcome the spring season, students at a university in Shandong province, China, painted tiny scenes on the insides of eggshells.

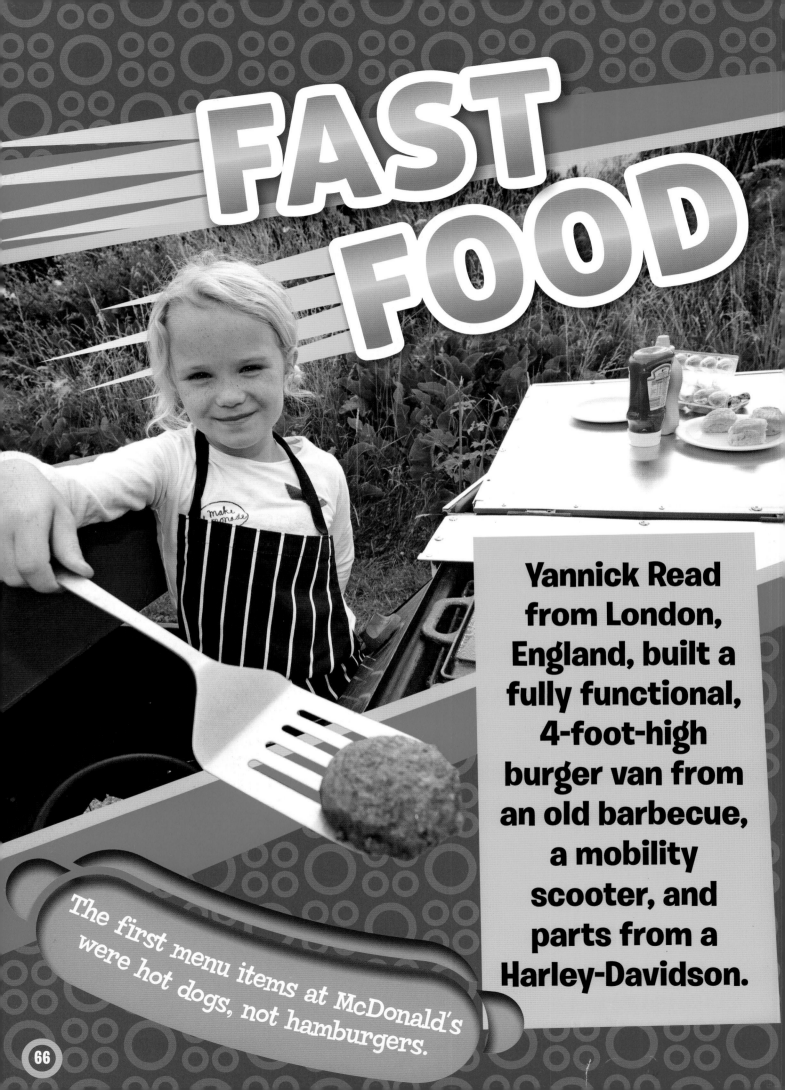

FAST FOOD

Yannick Read from London, England, built a fully functional, 4-foot-high burger van from an old barbecue, a mobility scooter, and parts from a Harley-Davidson.

The first menu items at McDonald's were hot dogs, not hamburgers.

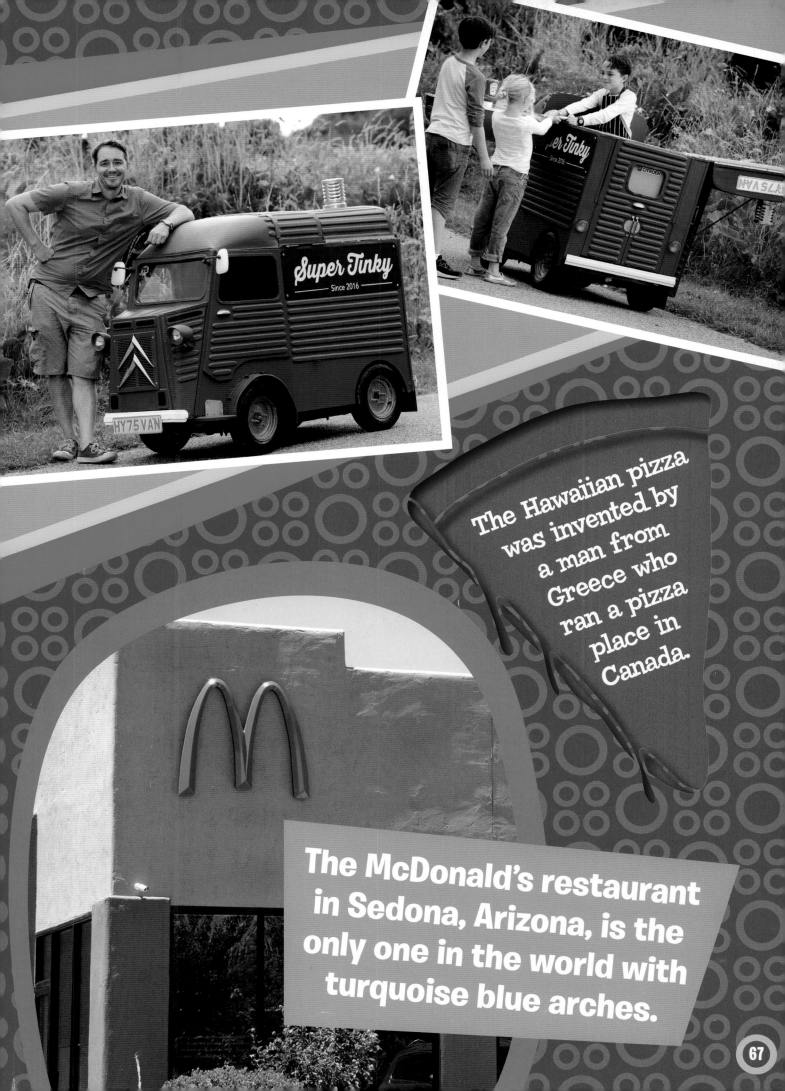

The Hawaiian pizza was invented by a man from Greece who ran a pizza place in Canada.

The McDonald's restaurant in Sedona, Arizona, is the only one in the world with turquoise blue arches.

Fast Food FIND

Find all 16 words hidden on the napkin! Make sure to look up, down, across, and diagonally!

chips

pizza

tacos

combo

hot dog

cheeseburger

bacon

fries

condiments

soda

menu

sandwich

milkshake

drive through

onion rings

nuggets

Write it here:

_____.

```
O R H N M S A C T P D D M Q M
S Q P W E F R I E S R O A F M
C A V F N G S Z M B I R U L I
H L L V U I A D K V V C D U L
E B G A C O N D I M E N T S K
E Q H S D N D J B X T U P B S
S Y Q U D I W E E A H H L N H
E C O M B O I X B G R O P C A
B T B R H N C W Z J O T I U K
U F U N X R H G S M U D Z O E
R T M S S I C M T Q G O Z N E
G B A O T N H D E T H G A M X
E U C D V G I L F M B A C O N
R A D A R S P U N U G G E T S
T G I U R M S G L W R Z Y K G
```

Want to see how you did?
Turn to pages 88-90 for the solutions!

NO EASY FEET

Chinese college student Peng Chao lost both of his arms as a child, so he plays video games with his feet!

He streams himself playing online so others can watch him play in real time.

GROWL COWL

Styles include red panda, orangutan, collie dog, lion, and even a mythical yeti!

Novelty apparel company Beardo makes ski masks that turn you into a wild animal!

73

TANGLED

Spiders tune the strings of their webs like a guitar!

Spiders recycle webs by eating them.

Most spiders are afraid of ants.

Only one species of spider, *Bagheera kiplingi*, is an herbivore.

Help the bee find its way out of the sticky web!

Want to see how you did?
Turn to pages 88-90 for the solutions!

A BREED

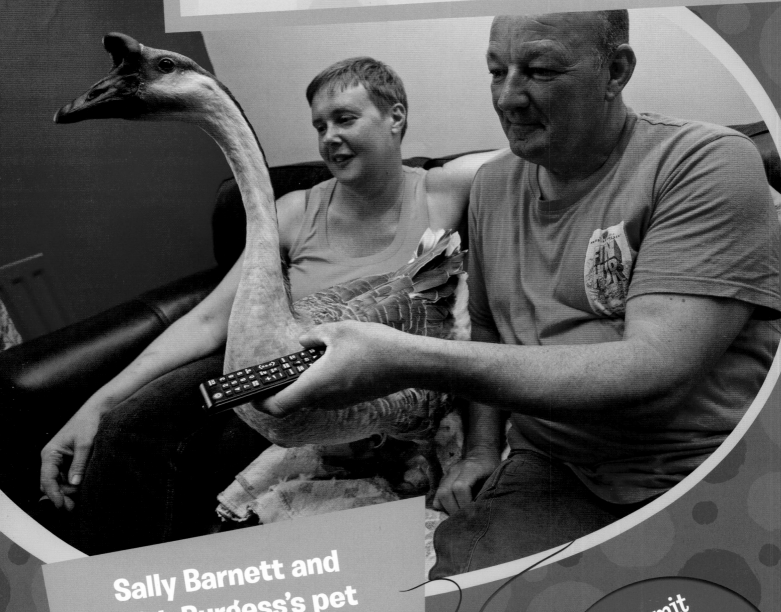

Sally Barnett and Keith Burgess's pet goose Jack lives in their Market Drayton, Shropshire, home with them and even enjoys watching TV!

Hermit crabs are actually social animals.

APART

Veterinarian Erika de Jager of Tsumeb, Namibia, adopted a baby aardvark after it was separated from its mother.

The aardvark's name is Gertie and she loves playing with her owner's pet dogs!

Can someone pass me a towel?

Take a Walk

Shoe designer Kobi Levi creates stilettos that look like animals—even flamingos!

Squish, an abandoned baby flamingo at Singapore's Jurong Bird Park, was fitted with a pair of handmade blue boots to protect its feet from the park's hot concrete.

Sneakers got their name because their rubber soles do not make noise.

The first pair of Nike running shoes was made in a waffle iron.

EGG-CELLENT

Michele Baldini of Monterrey, Mexico, uses eggs to create art in a frying pan!

One ostrich egg is equivalent to 24 chicken eggs.

Fill the frying pan with your own egg art!

Bon Appetit

A 26-foot-tall fork sticks out of Lake Geneva in Vevey, Switzerland.

Micronutris in France raises insects for eating and produces treats like these chocolates topped with crickets, which are said to crunch like puffed rice and taste like hazelnut.

Ketchup used to be sold in pill form as medicine!

Nothing in the Aufschnitt Textile Butchery in Berlin, Germany, is edible! Rather, everything is made out of cloth and stuffing, creating fun throw pillows for your home.

Mount Kilimanjaro

Lotus Temple

Forbidden City

Machu Picchu

Uluru

Mount Fuji

Egypt
China
India
Peru
Italy
Australia
Japan
United States
Jordan
Tanzania

Great Sphinx

Petra

Draw a line connecting these famous landmarks to their home country.

MONUMENT MATCH

Want to see how you did?
Turn to pages 88-90 for the solutions!

Grand Canyon

Leaning Tower of Pisa

Glow Up!

These multicolored beams, called "light pillars," in Moncton, New Brunswick, Canada, are naturally occuring and caused by rare atmospheric conditions.

Glow worms aren't actually worms!

This bike path in the Netherlands is lined with glow-in-the-dark stones!

The bones of certain chameleon species glow fluorescent under UV light!

Answers

Macaron Match   PAGE 19

Face the Music

PAGE 52

ARE YOU READY TO ROCK?

cake cute dare
duck race taco true

actor error radar
today

arcade carrot
create doctor
karate rocket
turkey

educate outdoor

88

Face the Music **PAGE 53**

One Fell Swoop

PAGE 62

One Fell Swoop

PAGE 63

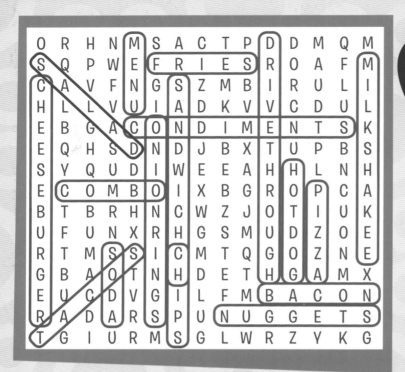

Fast Food Find

PAGE 69

Monument Match

PAGE 84

Great Sphinx	**Egypt**
Forbidden City	**China**
Lotus Temple	**India**
Machu Picchu	**Peru**
Mount Fuji	**Japan**
Uluru	**Australia**
Grand Canyon	**United States**
Petra	**Jordan**
Leaning Tower of Pisa	**Italy**
Mount Kilimanjaro	**Tanzania**

Tangled

PAGE 75

If you enjoyed *Play It Loud!*, you'll love the rest of the Fun Facts and Silly Stories series! Each book is filled with crazy facts, amazing tales, and, of course, tons of fun puzzles and games!

FUN FACTS Ripley's Believe It or Not! Kids & Silly Stories
THE BIG ONE!

Ripley's Believe It or Not! Kids & Silly Stories
ODD AROUND THE WORLD!

FUN FACTS Ripley's Believe It or Not! Kids & Silly Stories
ONE ZANY DAY!

FUN FACTS Ripley's Believe It or Not! Kids & Silly Stories
THE MANE EVENT!

Ripley's Believe It or Not! TIME WARP
The past and present collide!

If you have a fun fact or silly story, send it to us at bionresearch@ripleys.com

Get ready to have your mind warped by this incredible collection of events, inventions, and people that you won't believe existed at the same time in history!

Learning with a Ripley's twist! Engaging illustrations, silly characters, and fun-to-follow examples make these brand new board books the most unique thing in your little one's first book collection.

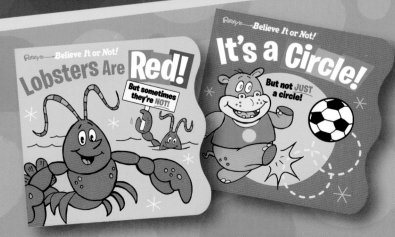

Ripley's Believe It or Not! Lobsters Are Red! But sometimes they're NOT!

Ripley's Believe It or Not! It's a Circle! But not JUST a circle!

ACKNOWLEDGMENTS

FRONT COVER © Aleksei Verhovski/Shutterstock.com; **BACK COVER** (t) © jaroslava V/Shutterstock.com, (c) © Kuttelvaserova Stuchelova/Shutterstock.com; **1** Melissa Huang (Instagram Account @mellyeatsworld) ; **2** (tl) Michele Baldini, "The Eggshibit", (bl) © F STOP IMAGES/Shutterstock.com; **3** (tl) Daniel Alex Todd, (c) © Elena Veselova/Shutterstock.com, (b) Claudio Baeggli/Null Stern/Caters News; **4** John S Lander/LightRocket via Getty Images; **5** (t) John S Lander/LightRocket via Getty Images, (b) John S Lander/LightRocket via Getty Images; **6** ADEK BERRY/AFP/Getty Images; **7** (t) Brill/ullstein bild via Getty Images, (c) Pigi Cipelli/Archivio Pigi Cipelli/Mondadori Portfolio via Getty Images, (b) © Benguhan/Shutterstock.com; **10-11** Stefan Pabst/REX/Shutterstock; **12-13** (dp) © geertweggen/Shutterstock.com; **12** (l) © Fascinadora/Shutterstock.com, (r) © Happy Art/Shutterstock.com; **13** (t) © Happy Art/Shutterstock.com; **14-15** (dp) © Andrea Izzotti/Shutterstock.com; **14** The Asahi Shimbun via Getty Images; **15** © Irina Klyuchnikova/Shutterstock.com; **16-17** (dp) © Big Pearl/Shutterstock.com; **16** Anders Tukler/Alamy Stock Photo; **17** ImagineChina; **18** Melissa Huang (Instagram Account @mellyeatsworld) ; **19** (br) © Martial Red/Shutterstock.com; **20** The Asahi Shimbun via Getty Images; **21** (t) ImagineChina, (b) Rick Madonik/Toronto Star via Getty Images, (bkd) © jajaladdawan/Shutterstock.com; **22** (t) © Production Perig/Shutterstock.com, (l) © Svietlieisha Olena/Shutterstock.com, (tr) © everydoghasastory/Shutterstock.com, (br) © Haland/Shutterstock.com; **23** (tl) © Victor Tyakht/Shutterstock.com, (tcl) © reptiles4all/Shutterstock.com, (bcl) © Iasha/Shutterstock.com, (bl) © Eric Isselee/Shutterstock.com, (tr) © Mvijit/Shutterstock.com, (br) © jaroslava V/Shutterstock.com; **24-25** (dp) Tobias Rodenkirch/Caters News; **25** Martin Knobel/Caters News; **26-27** Boaz Rottem; **27** (tr, br) © Mariya Isachenko/Shutterstock.com; **28-29** (dp) © gresei/Shutterstock.com; **28** © Elena Veselova/Shutterstock.com; **29** (c) © Elena Elisseeva/Shutterstock.com, (b) © Picsfive/Shutterstock.com; **30** (t) Pam Ishiguro/Barcroft Images/Barcroft Media via Getty Images, (b) © LYekaterina/Shutterstock.com; **31** (t) Keiko Otsuhata, (b) Michael J Cohen/Cover Images; **32** Christopher Horsley/Caters News; **33** (tl) NASA/Johns Hopkins University Applied Physics Laboratory/Carnegie Institution of Washington, (bl) NASA/JPL, (r) Public Domain/Erwan Mirabeau/Wikimedia Commons; **36** (bl) Claudio Baeggli/Null Stern/Caters News; **37** (tl) Caters News, (br) John Nguyen/JNVisuals/Cover Images; **38-39** (dp) YASUYOSHI CHIBA/AFP/Getty Images; **38** (bl) © Vdant85/Shutterstock.com; **39** Fabio Teixeira/Anadolu Agency/Getty Images; **40-41** © Mathis Dumas/Solent News & Photo Agency; **41** (t) Caters News, (b) Andrey Bazanov via SellYourPhoto.net; **42-43** (tr, tl, bl) Georgi Slavov via SellYourPhoto.net; **42** (br) © Lynne Nicholson/Shutterstock.com; **44-45** (dp) JTB MEDIA CREATION, Inc./Alamy Stock Photo; **45** (tl) © YU YUN-PING/Shutterstock.com, The Asahi Shimbun via Getty Images; **46-47** (dp) GARY WAINWRIGHT/CATERS NEWS; **46** GARY WAINWRIGHT/CATERS NEWS; **48-49** © Sky Antonio/Shutterstock.com; **50-51** (dp) © Wiktoria Matynia/Shutterstock.com; **50** (tl) © vetre/Shutterstock.com, (bl) © Ezzolo/Shutterstock.com, (tc) © argus/Shutterstock.com, (c) © Sonsedska Yuliia/Shutterstock.com, (tr) © Panos Karas/Shutterstock.com, (br) © Mega Pixel/Shutterstock.com; **51** (tr) © Sayers1/Shutterstock.com, (tc) © Wiktoria Matynia/Shutterstock.com, (c) © Creativa Images/Shutterstock.com, (bc) © Martial Red/Shutterstock.com, (bl) © xpixel/Shutterstock.com, (br) © Annette Shaff/Shutterstock.com; **52** (t) © Wiktoria Matynia/Shutterstock.com, (b) © F STOP IMAGES/Shutterstock.com; **54-55** (dp) DAVID OGDEN/CATERS NEWS; **54** (tl, cl) ImagineChina; **55** (tr) © Robert Kneschke/Shutterstock.com, (br) DAVID OGDEN/CATERS NEWS; **57** (t) JOSEPH EID/AFP/Getty Images; **58** (tl) Daniel Alex Todd, (bl) © browndogstudios/Shutterstock.com, (br) © LuckyVector/Shutterstock.com; **59** Matt Mertz/Caters; **60-61** (dp) © Imran Ashraf/Shutterstock.com; **60** (bl) © Eric Isselee/Shutterstock.com; **61** (tr) Cultura RM/Alamy Stock Photo, (br) © Lucie Rezna/Shutterstock.com; **64** (tl, cl, bl) Joanna Hedrick/Cover Images, (r) © Lana Tomberg/Shutterstock.com; **65** (t) John Kucko, (b) ImagineChina; **66** (t) Jonathan Hordle/REX/Shutterstock, (b) © Alex_Murphy/Shutterstock.com; **67** (tl) Jonathan Hordle/REX/Shutterstock, (tr) Jonathan Hordle/REX/Shutterstock, (c) © Sloth Astronaut/Shutterstock.com, (cl) © Sheila Fitzgerald/Shutterstock.com; **68-69** (dp) © Mariya Isachenko/Shutterstock.com; **68** (cl) © Davydenko Yuliia/Shutterstock.com, (cr) © Abramova Elena/Shutterstock.com; **69** (t) © Hans Geel/Shutterstock.com; **70-71** ImagineChina; **72-73** Kurt Thompson (Kurtogram) ; **74** KUTUB UDDIN/MERCURY PRESS via Caters News; **76** (t) Laura Dale/Caters News, (b) © ReachDreams/Shutterstock.com; **77** Caters News; **78** Caters News; **79** (l) REUTERS/Natasha Howitt, (tr) © I am Kulz/Shutterstock.com, (br) © AlenKadr/Shutterstock.com; **80-81** (dp) Michele Baldini, "The Eggshibit" ; **80** (bkd) © SedovaY/Shutterstock.com, (br) © Les Perysty/Shutterstock.com; **82-83** (dp) Patrick Aventurier/Getty Images; **82** © Roman Babakin/Shutterstock.com; **83** (t) © Mariya Isachenko/Shutterstock.com, (b) Avid Tal/Barcroft Images/Barcroft Media via Getty Images; **84** (tr) © saiko3p/Shutterstock.com, (tl) © Volodymyr Burdiak/Shutterstock.com, (tc) © zhengzaishuru/Shutterstock.com, (bc) © Allik/Shutterstock.com, (bl) © leodaphne/Shutterstock.com, (br) © onemu/Shutterstock.com; **85** (tl) © Pius Lee/Shutterstock.com, (tr) © NAPA/Shutterstock.com, (br) © Fedor Selivanov/Shutterstock.com, (bl) © Galyna Andrushko/Shutterstock.com; **86** Sophie Melanson; **87** (t) DAAN ROOSEGAARDE AND HEIJMANS/ CATERS NEWS, (b) David Protzel/ Caters News; **91** © Javier Brosch/Shutterstock.com; **MASTER GRAPHICS** © Artfull/Shutterstock.com, © Max Krasnov/Shutterstock.com, © Aleksei Verhovski/Shutterstock.com

Key: t = top, b = bottom, c = center, l = left, r = right, dp = double page, bkg = background

All other photos are from Ripley Entertainment Inc.

Every attempt has been made to acknowledge correctly and contact copyright holders, and we apologize in advance for any unintentional errors or omissions, which will be corrected in future editions.